— DENNIS MICHAEL VINCENT —

GOD
IS REAL IN MY LIFE

LifeRich Publishing is a registered trademark of The Reader's Digest Association, Inc.

LifeRich Publishing books may be ordered through booksellers or by contacting:

LifeRich Publishing
1663 Liberty Drive
Bloomington, IN 47403
www.liferichpublishing.com
1 (888) 238-8637

Because of the dynamic nature of the Internet, any web addresses or links contained in this book may have changed since publication and may no longer be valid. The views expressed in this work are solely those of the author and do not necessarily reflect the views of the publisher, and the publisher hereby disclaims any responsibility for them.

Any people depicted in stock imagery provided by Thinkstock are models, and such images are being used for illustrative purposes only. Certain stock imagery © Thinkstock.

ISBN: 978-1-4897-1020-8 (sc)
ISBN: 978-1-4897-1021-5 (hc)
ISBN: 978-1-4897-1019-2 (e)

Library of Congress Control Number: 2016921178

Print information available on the last page.

LifeRich Publishing rev. date: 01/24/2017

CONTENTS

CONTENTS

WHO AM I?

I have only one name and very few use it.

Most people avoid me. They do not want my presence.

Some people long for me and are waiting for my presence.

Some people get mad when I come in the room, others are happy.

Envy and jealousy try to drive people from me.

I bring fear to some people, trouble to others, and to some depression.

I hurt most people.

Most people are ashamed of me, but look for me every day and hope they do not find me.

Most people do not know what to do with me. I am too simple to understand.

God and Wisdom are the only ones that stand with me.

I am the answer to your questions.

When you look in the mirror, you will see me.

WHO AM I?

The answer
Second letter [it]
Second letter [they]
Second letter [people]
Next word

Second letter [other]
First letter [room]
Six letter [jealous]
First letter [try]
First letter [hope]

GOD IS REAL IN MY LIFE AND MY JOURNEY

DENNIS MICHAEL VINCENT

Three Diplomas in the Bible

Author and Co Author

Retired from G.M.

Vietnam, veteran

Married for forty eight years

Three children

Three Grandchildren

One Great Grandchild

Honorary member of the Genesee
T.W.P. Firefighter Association

HOW I GOT SAVED

When I was eighteen years old, God chased me down and I got saved. The Sundays of my youth were not spent in a church building. Most would say I never went to church having only attended about twelve times during my childhood. Instead of knowing God, I ran from him. I was mad at the world. I hated school. My vocabulary consisted of many curse words. I was going down the wrong road. Then one day I hit a detour. Thank God for the detour.

Here is my story beginning sometime back in 1965...

While at school, my friends pointed out a teacher. They told me that he played cards and drank with students. This sounded like a good time, so two weeks later I approached him and asked him to attend our party. He said that he couldn't make it because he "would be praising the Lord."

I apologized immediately, and told him my friends must have been setting me up. He assured me they weren't. He indeed was that person, up until a week prior. He had just given his life to the Lord and was changing his ways. As I went to leave he invited me to the church he was attending down the road. I left knowing I was not going to meet him at his church.

Twice in the next few weeks I ran into this teacher in town. Every time he told me he didn't see me at church and invited me again. Prior to our first interaction, I don't recall seeing this man around. Now, suddenly, he was everywhere. It turned out he had just moved into my neighborhood. To appease him I told him I would go along if he picked me up. I was fairly certain he would forget. On Sunday night when there was a knock on my door I was shocked. I reluctantly went along thinking that if I went this one time he would stop pestering me.

The church he took me to was not the one in the neighborhood that he had mentioned during our first encounter. At the end of service when he asked me how I liked it I simply told him it wasn't the church, I thought we would be attending. I thought perhaps he decided he didn't like that church so I agreed to go the next week if we went to the neighborhood church. Again, I didn't think the teacher would show up. However, he did. He told me if that was the church I preferred he would go with me. I told him if he missed a week that was it, game over, no more church. So for six weeks, every Sunday night, there was the teacher at my door ready to take me to church.

By week seven I decided I was done with church. I took my mother to get groceries so I wouldn't be home before church started. My mother and I got home at 7:20 that was twenty minutes after the service had started. I thought I was golden, I was out. But then I heard a knock at the door. The teacher was there. It turned out he was running late himself, but knew we could still make it for the preaching part of service. The first amazing part of that night was he didn't know I was trying to avoid him. The second amazing part was that the church service was running late. When we got there they hadn't even started. As far as I know, never in this church's history past to present have they ever ran thirty minutes late. However, that night they did. It was as if it they were waiting, waiting for me personally.

As, I was leaving the church that evening the pastor approached me.

He said, "I thought you were going to get saved tonight." I told him I thought that I was too.

Then he said the words that changed my life, "It isn't too late."

It wasn't too late, it is never too late. That evening I walked into a Sunday school classroom, I knelt down, and I asked Jesus into my life. God has been a part of my life ever since that day.

Hebrews 10:31, It is a fearful thing to fall into the hands of the living God.

My ministries over the years have consisted of....

- Preaching at my place of employment
- Handing out over 5,000 New Testaments
- Handing out over 1,000 Bibles
- Handing out over 400 Books of John
- Occasionally Preaching
- Officiating Wedding Ceremonies

THE LIFE OF A CHRISTIAN

God will be real in your life.
It is not an easy road to go down.
Jesus said what they have done to me;
they will also do unto you.
You might lose all of your family. [Will
not like what you are doing]
All your friends will be gone. [Will not want you around]
People in the Bible; end up in jail for taking a stand for Jesus
Beat to death for taking a stand for Jesus
People will talk bad about you.
Kill you
It might be just you and Jesus at times or all the time.
Blessings will come to you for all of your trying times.
This is where Faith comes into the picture.
There will be times when you do not know why things
are going all wrong. Then later you will see why God
did what he did and then sometimes we do not see it.
Some things are hard to understand, no matter
what is happing, God is in control.
There are times when it does not look like it.
We do not understand why God does what he does.
There are a whole lot of these things in the Bible.
Different people in the Bible go through some hard
times and bad times. Some lose loved ones.

The more time you spend with God, the more He
will tell you about himself and His ways.

God is not a light switch, you can turn on and off, He is
not a toy you pick up and play with when you feel like it.
Jesus is God, He is there to help you, all the
way, and give you everything you want.

Jesus let this person feel your presence
when they read this book. Amen

May God deeply bless you and your family

Dennis Michael Vincent

THIS IS GOD'S BOOK

All of my materials come from Jesus Himself and the Book of the Bible King James Version, Old and New Testament

Colossians 1:9 For this cause we also, since the day we heard it, do not cease to pray for you, and to desire that ye might be filled with the knowledge of his will in all wisdom and spiritual understanding;

10 That ye might walk worthy of the Lord unto all pleasing, being fruitful in every good work, and increasing in the knowledge of God;

MY LIFE AND A SHORT STORY OF A FEW MIRACLES I WITNESSED

I WENT TO BIBLE SCHOOL

Back in the day, a lot of kids never went to school. They had to work on the farm. My dad was one of those kids. He could work but he could not write or read. Back then, all he had to do was make an X and that was good enough for his signature. Then everything changed. He had to write his name to get his check cashed. My sister spent hundreds of hours trying to teach my dad how to write his name. She thought he would never learn.

My mother went to school just enough to learn how to read and write. There were six of us, three girls and three boys. I was the youngest. My sisters were having babies when I came along. They all dropped out of school. I was their only hope to have one make it. I did not do well in school. I went through the fifth grade twice and had to pass summer school if I wanted to go to high school. I got my diploma by the skin of my teeth. Mom and dad were happy.

Married with two kids, the third child was born eight years later .Trying to make ends meet. God laid it on my heart to go to Bible school. Because I did very poorly in school, I did not run right down there and sign up. Four years later the wife and I went down to a Bible institute and asked if they would accept me as a student. I knew a college would not take me, but this was a Bible institute, not a college. With my poor learning skills, they still could have turned me down.

The President of the school said, "You really don't qualify to come to this school with the grades you got in school. Why do you want to come to my school?"

I said, "I do not know anything about the Bible and I want to know all about what is in this Book."

The President asked, "Do you want to be a preacher, or a teacher or a missionary or do some other kind of work for the Lord"?

I said, "No, I just want to learn what is in this Book." The President asked, "Do you know anything about the Bible"? I said, "No, nothing."

The President said, "Come back in two weeks and talk to the Vice President. He will make the final decision on this."

Two weeks later my wife and I were talking to the Vice President, He asked "What brings you to the school?"

I answered, "God laid it on my heart to go to Bible school." Vice President asked, "To be what a preacher, a teacher, what did He want you to do for Him?"

I replied, "I do not want to be anything. I just want to know what is in the Book. You teach the Bible here, right?"

The Vice President, said, "Yes but,"

I responded, "Hey, you are letting me off the hook with God. I did not want to come here in the first place. I feel better already; it is between you and God. There for a while I thought God was going to make me go to school again. Thanks a lot."

The Vice President said, "You do not qualify to be in this school but I will let you in and I will keep an eye on you and help you get through all of this."

I struggled for fifteen years, I made it. Forty years later, I know the Bible frontwards and backwards. I got it. Jesus gave it all to me. I can talk the Bible all day and I do not even have to open it up.

God called me to write for him. I told him no, I do not know how to spell and put words on paper to make sense. Two years later, I gave up and started writing for him. I sent out my writing to over four hundred preachers and the preachers did not like what I wrote. I had God confirm what He gave me three times. I like to fish by myself and all three of these signs came while I was fishing. When the fish are not biting, I think and talk to God about what He gave me to write about.

I took my granddaughter fishing one day. The fish were biting so fast, I just laid my pole down and the bait went in the water. While I was baiting her hook, a fish came up, taking the bait and my fishing pole into the water. I told my granddaughter the only way I could get the fishing pole back was if God brought it back. Two hours later, my granddaughter said, "Grandpa I see your bobber under the water." I looked and there it was. I took her fishing pole, hooked the line just behind the bobber and pulled my fishing pole out of the water. I told her don't worry about the fish. I will take it off and then something strange happened; the fish spit the hook and swam away. It was like the fish had said here is your fishing pole back.

It was hard to believe that God brought my fishing pole back. I never saw anything like this before.

Another day, I was out fishing and they were not biting. I asked the Lord, "If what I was writing was from Him or from me?"

I said, "The preachers think it is me and not you Lord. I want you to show me a sign. I want you to let me catch a cat fish 28 inches long."

I did not catch the cat fish. I was broken hearted over this. God did not give me the fish. I did not tell anybody what I said to God.

A week later, a man from the church stopped by and said, "I want you to go fishing with me over in Port Huron, Michigan in a river that comes into Lake Huron." We had to drive around 70 miles to get there. We were fishing for about one hour, when I hooked into a big one. It took me 15 minutes to land it. A stranger had to net it for me. I gave him the fish; it was a cat fish 28 inches long. I never said anything to them about what I said to the Lord. I just thanked the Lord under my breath.

Another day, we were visiting my granddaughter in Jacksonville, Florida, when my wife fell and broke her left hip. Two years before she had broken her right hip, she was in rehab for three weeks. There was a lake next to the parking lot. I told her I was going to go fishing in the lake. She said that would do me good. I had been in to see her for the past 15 days. I went to Wal-Mart and bought a kid's fishing pole. I opened it up at the hotel room and the line would not come out so I tried to fix it. For some reason I could not fix it. So the next day, I took it back and got an adult fishing pole. Now I can catch a big fish. While I was fishing, I told the Lord if I was on the same page with Him, let me catch a big fish. Five minutes later, I hooked into a big fish. He was really fighting then he stopped. The drag was to loose and I could not reel him in. I did not know what to do. I did not want to break the line. After a minute, I tried pulling the line in with my hand a little at a time. I took in the line as I pulled it. It worked. The fish was getting closer. I finally got it. The fish was a 22 inch Bass. I took the fish in and showed my wife. She said she had only seen fish that big on TV.

I asked for another sign from God concerning my writings of David and Bathsheba.

Some preachers put the blame on Bathsheba for committing adultery with David. My writing

Confirms her innocence because she was raped by David.

My son and I passed out fifty copies of my writings on the way to the ball game.

Here is the story. My youngest son stops by one day and said, we will go see the New England Patriots play their first football game for the season. We could not get tickets to the game. We tried for thirty days. No Luck. Now we are going to drive one thousand miles to a football game that has been sold out for 30 days. I told my son we would pass out my writings on David raping Bathsheba. If it is true, we want into the ball game. If it is not true, do not let us into the ball game. We passed out over fifty copies on the way. We wanted God to Know we meant business. Nobody at the hotel had any tickets. If you get to the Lions game at ten A.M. you will be the only people there. They started coming in around eleven A.M. to eleven forty five A.M. We arrived there at ten A.M. The place was packed. It looked like it was eleven A.M I asked my son if our watches were wrong. He said no. I pulled in to park the man said that will be forty dollars. I told my son I will not pay forty dollars to park if we don't have tickets. The man said turn around and go up to McDonalds, that was easier said than done .We had to pull into a bar, nobody was in his parking lot. The cars were at a dead stop and McDonalds was 3 blocks down the road. We asked the man if we could park here until we could get some tickets. He said no, then he said one of us could go and one could stay, so my son left to get tickets. I put a tape in and he came back before the second song was over. I said, do you have the tickets he said no. But we can park next door for twenty dollars.

How are we going to get tickets? We have to make a sign. We took the top of the box that was filled with the writings on David Raping Bathsheba. My son made a sign. We need two tickets. He just got the sign up and two people pulled in one person had one ticket the other person had two tickets. We told the one driver we were going with the man that had two tickets. The man said my daughter and her friend could not make it to the game today. I saw your sign. These tickets are season tickets the cost is one hundred dollars a ticket. We were planning on spending one hundred dollars a ticket anyways. We bought the tickets. I will see you at the game. It was around eleven forty five A.M. God answered our prayer. We knew, David, raped Bathsheba. Not only did GOD get us in the ballgame. But we had the best seats in the Stadium.

There were only four seats in this Stadium with this man's name on it. My son and I were sitting in two of them. We were scared to death. Things like this just do not happen. We knew God did this for us. God gave me my sign.

New England won and they went on to win the Super Bowl that year.

Hebrews 10:31 It is a fearful thing to fall into the hands of the living God.

SOME SHORT STORIES

THE COFFEE BREAK

Some times at work I would sit down and have a cup of coffee with the guys. One day, I sat down with two guys, one was a drunk and the other was a pot head. They never talked to me again and this is why.

The drunk asked, "Preacher, what is going on? The Lord's blessings are falling on me. The pot head and I think the Lord is blessing us more than you."

I said, "I'm going to buy me a bottle and a bag of dope tonight."

The drunk said, "It is about time you got on track with us."

I said, "Maybe you guys can help me out here about my big journey of sin. I'm about to go on". The drunk said, "What is it you want to know preacher? You know the pot head and me know all about this stuff."

I asked, "Here is the question, how long do I have to look at the bottle of booze before I get drunk?"

The drunk said, "Are you feeling all right preacher? Everybody knows you got to open the bottle and drink it. Feel his head pot man make sure the preacher doesn't have a fever."

I asked, "Pot man, how long do I have to look, at the pot before I get the buzz on?"

The pot man said, "Preacher you are not making any sense. Everybody knows you cannot look at pot and get a buzz on; you have to open the bag and smoke it. I think it is time for you to leave preacher."

The drunk said, "You better leave preacher, you and all of your stupidity today. What did you do? Did you take a stupid pill today?"

I said, "Let me tell you something before I leave."

The pot head said "Make it quick."

I said, "Mr. Drunk, just because you have a Bible in your house does not mean God is blessing you. You have to open it, read it, and hang on to it just like that bottle. Then the blessings of God will fall on you. Mr. Pot man just because you sit around and talk about God does not mean you are on your way to Heaven. You have to open your heart and ask Jesus to come into your heart and spend as much time with God as you do with that dope. You guys have a good day."

The drunk and dope head said at the same time, "Preacher don't you ever talk to us again".

EUROPEAN VACATION

My oldest Son said, "Dad I want to go to a Christian school for my high school years." I moved my kids over to the Christian School. This school took their seniors to Europe for their senior trip. The kids worked and paid their own way. They stayed at Youth Hostels; they are like the Y. M. C. A.

They saw around eight countries each year. They had their own bus and tour guide. In 1998, the school sent me a letter that said we were invited to go to Europe with them. They were taking the parents of the kids that graduated from their school. The wife and I went. We visited seven countries France, Luxembourg, Germany, Czech Republic, Austria, Liechtenstein, and Switzerland.

Here are two strange stories that happened to us.

THE HARD ROCK CAFÉ,

My wife and I have eaten in forty seven Hard Rock Cafés. Ten of them have been out of the U.S.A. My youngest son collects the shot glasses they sell. Looking for the Hard Rock Café in Paris France was going to be like looking for a needle in a hay stack. The wife and I agreed not to try to find it. When we came out of the bank from getting our money exchanged, we saw a man walking down the street wearing a Hard Rock Café tee shirt. We asked the man where he purchased that shirt. He spoke English and said three blocks down the street. We said, Are you sure?

He said, "It was there yesterday."

We were pleasantly surprised that we found the Hard Rock Café. We were able to purchase the glass for our son.

When we were in the city of Prague, Czech Rep. My wife and I got lost. We were trying to find our way back to where we started. A real nice looking woman hollered at me. I looked over at her and she waved her hand to tell me to come to her. I went over to her, she ask in English, "Are you lost? Here is a map to help you find your way back." She showed me where I was on the map. We found our way back.

Here are two strange things that have happened to us, while we were on vacation.

Hebrews 13:2 KJV Be not forgetful to entertain strangers: for thereby some have entertained angels unawares.

We were in South Carolina, in the summer time. It was 90 degree at 7 A.M. in the morning. No one was wandering around outside and there was not any traffic. I missed my turn. Waiting at a 5 minute red light, I could see that if I drove around this restaurant, I could miss this red light. I could make my right turn and be back on the right road again. I went around the restaurant; and I stopped to look before I made my turn. There was nobody on the road. Somebody started hitting my car. I asked the kids, "Who is hitting my car?"

They said, "An old lady with a full length, fur coat on with a big box under her arm."

I said, "Ask her what she wants."

She needed a ride to McDonald's. I tried to talk her out of it, but I finally gave in and took her three blocks down to McDonald's.

She said, "I want to go to the other McDonald's." We took her to the other McDonald's as she had asked. It was 15 miles down the road. I told the kids to keep an eye on her. They said she went in and they could not see her any more.

This was so strange, God brought to my mind Hebrews 13:2

On a separate occasion, we were on our way back from a Disney vacation. When we went to McDonald's to eat lunch, we were having a good time talking about our vacation. My wife did not go to Animal kingdom with us. I was telling her about the woman who explained about the Ape. She said the Ape does not have finger prints; the Ape has a mark on their nose for a print. When she got done telling us about the Ape, I told the woman to come closer to me. When she got next to me, I said maybe we did come from Apes. It looks like you have a mark on your nose. She laughed so hard she bent over. She laughed for a good 5 minutes. She said I have given that speech over 1,000 times and no one has ever said that. It tickled me that she laughed so hard. I started laughing too. My wife enjoyed the memory.

After leaving McDonald's, God saved my family from getting blown up with a gas truck.

I told my family that I was going to get gas before I get back on the road. When I got inside to pay for the gas, I had a hunger pain that hit me. So I bought 2 hot dogs. When I got back in the car, my family said, "What are you doing? You just ate."

I said, "I know that but I had this hunger pain hit me." They sat there for 20 minutes and watched me eat. They were not having a good time now. We got back on the road. We ran into a detour. I asked the man, "What was going on?"

He said, "If you would have been here 20 minutes earlier, you would have blown up with that gas truck."

Thank you Jesus for the hunger pain, which brought to my mind, Hebrews 10:31 KJV

It is a fearful thing to fall into the hands of the living God.

CATS

We went to New York City for my daughter's graduation gift. While we were there, we went and saw a Broadway play called Cats. We inquired about the story of Cats. Everyone said it is just about a lot of cats. We bought the program, so we could understand what the musical Cats was all about. The program said it was all about cats. Most programs explain the story line of the play. The Cats program did not explain the story line. We only bought the program to gain clarity about Cats. We were still in a fog about the story line of Cats. We asked, "Do you have another program?"

They said, "No"

We said, "Ok. We are sorry. We do not come to the city very often."

Then we proceeded to watch the play, Cats.

Much to our surprise, this play was all about GOD. It was a parable about Cats.

What's a parable? ; Simple story illustrating a moral truth.

The Main Cat in the play was named Deuteronomy.

Deuteronomy is the Fifth book in the Bible

These words are in the first song. Jellicles Can and Jellicles Do.

Heaviside layer, which Means heaven, Heaven and hell, Pieces from the Messiah

[Two times] Jesus is the Messiah, Hallelujah [Two times] the highest praise to God.

Mystical, Spiritual, relating to direct communion with God, Divinity Relating to or being God or a God

The rest of the play explains the first song.

Other words in the rest of the songs

Reborn, Rejoice that is where the new life begins, what happiness is, the last song.

The Mystical Divinity of unashamed felinity round the Cathedral rang vivat everlasting Cat

God had his say on Broadway for eighteen years.

A DATE WITH GOD

AUGUST 2014

My wife has been seriously ill for the past two and a half years. She suffers from a chronic pain condition called Trigminal Neuralgia that affects the trigminal nerve in the face and neck. This condition, along with other health issues has caused her to be in and out of hospitals and nursing homes for years. There have been three separate occasions when she has almost died. One time, in fact, they told us there was nothing they could do and thought she would pass away. For a last hope, we took her to a hospital in South Carolina for treatment. There she received two treatments. The plan was, if she was not better, we would return in six months' time for a third treatment. So six months later, still ill, we were on our way back to the hospital in South Carolina. The journey there would hit many more bumps than anticipated.

Because my wife is from North Carolina, we decided to stop at her home town on our way to the hospital. The day before we were to leave North Carolina for South Carolina, my wife fell. Falling when you are well is bad enough, but falling when you are already ill, that is not good. Sure enough, she had broken her hip. An ambulance took us to the hospital. Once there it was also discovered that my dear wife was wheezing and an x-ray was ordered. The results were not good either. The nurse informed me that my wife was in serious condition. She had congestive heart failure. She would need to be hooked up to a breathing machine and moved to a bigger hospital in Greensboro, N.C. or she could die within hours. I had to go to the hotel and get our belongings and then find my way back to the hospital. I was very lost but God helped me find my way and kept me calm in the midst of chaos.

Once I finally reached the hospital I had difficulty finding the entrance, the floor, and which room my wife was in. There was construction and it felt like every step was a hurdle when I just needed to get to my wife. When I reached her room sitting out front was the doctor. He told me he was about to take my wife for emergency surgery or she would not survive. I called my children, they told me to let the doctor operate.

So many things needed to be done. My oldest son needed to fly to North Carolina. We needed a hotel. God handled it all. After one call my son had a flight out within three hours. The hotel room was the last one available. The hotel location was also a straight shot to the hospital, no getting lost like the day before.

When my son arrived, we immediately went to see his mother. She was in a special wing of the ICU with ten rooms. They said that the people in this area were there to die. Five days is the longest they live. They said if she lives, she would be the first. My son has some medical background so he knew how to read the chart. It made me feel better and as though God was working through my son to help me understand exactly what was going on with my wife.

The rules of this wing of the hospital were no eating, drinking, or napping in the room. Also, when the doctor was on the floor, all visitors were required to leave for three hours. So when the doctor came, we had to leave.

Three hours later at our return, the nurse informed us that the doctor had said we could stay in the room with my wife at all times. We could eat, drink, nap, and be there when the doctors were in the room. God was helping us through this ordeal giving us favor in the eyes of the hospital staff. I knew that I needed a good night sleep in a bed not a chair in the hospital room so I had my son drive me back to the hotel. I had been awake for 37 hours at this point.

The next morning as I was heading out to the hospital, the hotel maintenance man asked me what I was doing in North Carolina. I told him about my wife. He started shaking his head with his mouth wide open. He told me that this is the week that every year is completely sold out. There shouldn't have been a room available for me, but there was. Thanks be to God, he knew we were coming. Not only did we manage to find a room when everything was sold out but we were given an amazing price too, almost half of what the other hotels cost.

The first fifteen days in the hospital were touch and go. The Lord saw us through it all. My son and I rotated eighteen hour shifts at the hospital. I would do eighteen hours, and then he would do eighteen hours. As things improved, we would trade off days and who went to the hotel at night. We were just trying to make it ourselves.

Three days into this ordeal, the doctor told us they needed to do surgery on her hip so she would be able to walk if she lives. My wife had sixteen IV's hooked up to her so preparing her for surgery took 45 minutes. During the procedure they couldn't put her under. They were afraid she would not wake up so she had a nurse sitting with her to make sure she was okay.

Thank God, the surgery went well. Slowly IVs were removed. Day after day the number dropped until she was down to eight. My son reassured me this was a positive sign. We made it fourteen more days of touch and go but in the end we won, my wife won. Praise the Lord.

We kept our faith but it wasn't always easy. Three weeks in, my son hit an all-time low. He needed some extra support, something I couldn't give. He was spending the afternoon away from the hospital when God led him to an all- Black barber shop for a haircut. They told him the white barber shop was next door. My son said I am in the right barber shop. While in the chair people in the shop started asking him where he was from and what he was doing in town. He told the story of his mother's illness and battle. Without having to ask for any support the barbers all stopped working and came over to pray with him. As they finished cutting his hair the shop erupted with praise songs. When his cut was done the barber told him the haircut was on them and that they would continue to pray that God would intervene. This was God, lifting my son up when he needed it most with complete strangers in the oddest of location.

God found ways to support us so many times while we were in North Carolina. Some things were small and may seem insignificant but when you are emotionally exhausted, those small things matter. At one restaurant we put our name in for a table. They were very busy and we were told the wait would be long. We decided to find somewhere else to go but then the hostess called our name and sat us right away. Another restaurant we asked to sit in the party room alone. We told the hostess about my wife. The next time we came in she recognized us and sat us in the party room again. Another family came in and demanded to sit in the back where we were but she knew we needed the quiet and didn't let them disturb us. Everywhere we went people would ask why we were in town, once we explained God would put it in their hearts to help us, to make everything a little easier on us.

Finally it came time to take my wife home. First my son had to take a couple of tests to show he knew how to care for her properly for the drive home. He passed both tests with ease since he is nearly a paramedic and we had spent so much time at the hospital watching and helping. In order to come home we needed five tanks of oxygen and a catheter. We signed mountains of paperwork. We were ready to go. I was worried. That is when God lightened the mood with a little comic relief. I was searching everywhere for my wife's teeth. We needed them before we left. The nurses were looking; they even called the other hospital's ER. Then a nurse came into the room and asked if we had looked in my wife's mouth. Sure enough, there they were. We had a good laugh and some of my stress was eased.

The day before leaving God was working too. I had a meltdown; the burden of taking my wife home was just too much. How would we manage? How would we even get her home with all the equipment she would require. My son decided to let me stay at the hotel to compose myself while he went to the hospital. He told me he would pick me up at five. We would both spend the day trying to figure out how to get everything and everyone home. Around 2pm the Lord laid on my heart to head downstairs at 4:30pm. There was no reason to be downstairs thirty minutes before my son would be there, but I felt like it was where God wanted me to be. Minutes later God sent his sign. A U-Haul trailer pulled up. I was so clouded with anxiety this option had not occurred to me, I needed God to put it there in front of my face. A few minutes after that my son pulled up and I told him I figured it out! We called U-Haul and thirty short minutes later we were set for how to get everything home. Thank you, Jesus we were able to pack up, get my wife, and head home that night.

As we left the doctor told us if my wife had not fallen and broken her hip we wouldn't have known about the breathing issue and she would have died within days. Even in adversity the Lord sends his support.

As for the treatment we were headed to in South Carolina, she did finally have it. The procedure is called Gamma Knife. It helps with the pain but wasn't able to completely take it away. My wife has good days and bad days. No matter what the day brings, we praise the Lord because she is still here.

YO-YO, CLOWN, AND PUPPETS

The yo-yo was all the rage when I was seven years old. Every year a man came around my town doing yo-yo tricks and had a contest. I wanted to win the contest so badly, but couldn't. This made me angry, but I turned my anger into a tool to push me. I spent the winter practicing my yo-yo skills. I knew come spring, I would win the contest. The man didn't come that year, or the next. Finally, when I was twelve he returned. I had kept up my yo-yo skills and was ready for his contest. The prize was a bike. I ended the day with a new bike! I thought that was the high-light of my yo-yo days, I had no idea that God would later use this skill to minister to children.

When I was half-way through Bible School my wife and I were at a meeting where a puppet show was put on. We were so impressed and thought that this was an area we could be involved with at our church. The children agreed that they wanted to be part of a puppet team and wanted me to be a clown and do yo-yo tricks. Yo-Yo the clown was born! It took a year and a half to raise the money needed for all of the equipment and to train the kids how to operate the puppets. During this time we hit many hurdles. The cost for everything was higher than we imagined it would be. Training to work puppets properly was grueling for the children. One of our first shows was at another church. Once we finished, the pastor got up and preached for thirty minutes about how puppets weren't real. That was discouraging. Turning myself into a clown proved challenging as well. I had yo-yo tricks, but I didn't know how to apply clown make-up. However, we persevered, knowing we were following God's will.

It felt as though God brought in all the right people at the right times to help us. So I kept on believing knowing I was following his direction for my life. While at a VA party making balloon animals for children a man approached me and handed me a phone number to a man who would help me perfect my clown appearance.

When we were fund raising the money was enough to cover everything. Many times seemed as though the events were set in motion by God; chance encounters, an uplifting word at just the right moment, a skill I learned as a seven year old child... God was with us.

We put on puppet shows until the children were out of school. After that, it was just too difficult. Being a puppeteer seems easy to the observer, but there is so much behind the scenes work that people don't realize. Even through the hard work we praised God. After the shows children would come forward and give their lives to the Lord. Eight children saved at one show, four at another, two at another.... we were doing the Lord's work and it was proving beneficial. We had fun and the Lord received the praise.

GOD IS REAL

A lot of things have happened in my life.
I'll tell you about three of them.

THE FIRST-

For five years I was a church bus driver. Each Sunday I picked up between fifteen and twenty kids. One year, I felt as though the Lord lay on my heart to give away a turkey for Thanksgiving. So I used a bingo ball system and drew a winner. The winner was a preacher boy, wife, and their two children. This family never rode the bus but did that day. I didn't understand why God would let them win. I felt as though they weren't in need like the regular riders. My wife and I were just sick over it.

About three years later my wife ran into that preacher boy's wife. The woman told my wife that she did not know why they rode the bus that day; she surely did not know a turkey was to be given away. She told my wife that they did not have the ability to purchase a turkey for Thanksgiving that year and had planned on going without. She thanked my wife for allowing them to have a Thanksgiving when they were certain they wouldn't that year.

THE SECOND-

God blessed me with a $1,000 bonus. Out of nowhere, I had a strong feeling that I needed to buy a sewing machine. I don't sew, my wife doesn't sew, and it made no sense. We had seen an ad in the paper for a huge sewing machine sale but what would we do with this machine? Each day it grew heavier on my heart to buy a sewing machine. I called our pastor, who is also the head of a Christian school, to see if he knew of someone in need of a sewing machine. Sure enough, the teacher who taught sewing at the school was in need of four machines and had been praying that somehow God would intervene since the school could not afford to purchase them. Because there was a sale machines that were originally $800 were now just over $200, so I bought all four machines for the school. God sent me that $1,000 because he knew I would listen when he called.

THE THIRD-

Luggage was the gift my mother gave me for graduation. I appreciated them but told her I didn't think I would ever use them. She told me, "You never know."

You never do know. Two years after high school I married a woman form North Carolina. Her mother had died when she was just 16, so her marrying me and moving away was very hard on her father. So began the first use of my luggage, going to visit my father-in-law.

The Lord continued to bless my life with the ability to travel with my family. My wife and I have been to fifteen countries and two cruises. My oldest boy has been to eight countries. My daughter has visited ten countries, one of which with us. My youngest son has visited five countries, three of which with us. My children were able to have a wonderful childhood full of travel. When we go on vacation we do as much as we can. We go, go, go, and then go some more! They saw more in a week of vacation than most see in a lifetime, no joke. We know so many people who never get to experience vacations. We are blessed, so when we travel to a new place we act as if we will never make it there again and experience everything we possibly can.

On top of vacations we are big sports fans, particularly the Tigers, Lions, and Pistons. We have been blessed with the ability to attend many games. We don't just take our family but are able to organize large groups so that other children, who may not be able to see a sports team play in person, can. I have taken four groups of thirty kids to games. Three were from church and one was a Cub Scout group.

My parents didn't take me on vacations or to sporting events. They didn't come out to cheer me on when I played sports. However, I was able to do that for my children and other peoples' children. To live a life that impacts others in a positive way is what I know God wants. He allowed me the resources to accomplish this because I listen to him when he speaks to me.

Growing in the Lord, here are some subjects that you should come to know more about over the years after you have been saved by grace.

GOD'S WAYS AND WHAT I'VE LEARNED OVER THE YEARS

God is in control of all matters, otherwise He is not God.
We don't understand everything that happens in our lives, if we did, we would be God.
The people in the Bible did not understand everything in their life.
A lot of this is about faith and sin.
The Bible says God's ways and man's ways are not alike.
God has one thing in mind and we have something else.
The more time you spend with God the more you will get out of God.
God wants to give you all your wants and desires.

Read the Bible and find out what God does in everyday life.
God does not leave us, we leave God out of our life, when something bad happens, we want God to fix it, right now.

ANGELS

Note
Jesus created man and Angels they are two different creations.
Man can have sex to multiply.
Jesus said angels do not have sex and Angels do not multiply.
Angels do not have sex with women. This is one thing Angels cannot do.
St. Matthew: 22 verse 30

HOLY SPIRIT

The Holy Spirit comes and goes in the Old Testament. The Holy Spirit came and went with Jesus. That's why he prays to the Father. After Jesus, was raised from the dead. The Holy Spirit comes and lives in your heart, when you get saved. And with faith Jesus said, we can move mountains.

LAW

God spoke the law before the flood.
God wrote the law with Moses.
After Jesus was raised from the dead, we preach the law under grace.
During the 1,000 year reign, we will teach the law.

LAND

God promised Abraham the land.
Israel never possesses all of the land. Judges 1:29-31

During the 1,000 year reign, Israel will get all the land promised to Abraham.

ISRAEL

In a nut shell
Adam, Noah, Abraham,
Jacob name change to Israel, [Genesis chapter 36 verse10]
Jesus and Israel, Gentiles and Israel,
Israel, teaching the world the law
Israel became a Nation in 1948

ISRAEL

You will go to jail and you may never get
out, if you preach Jesus in Israel.
It is against the law to have a church
in Israel and preach Jesus.
If you were to tell somebody about
Jesus and they told on you.
You are going to jail.
Israel rejected Jesus as God and they still do.

GENTILES

Jesus said on the cross, "It is finished" Jesus divorced Israel.
When Jesus was raised from the dead. Israel dies and is still dead 2016.
Jesus adopts the Gentiles.
Gentile's time will end, at the time, Jesus will call for the church.
Then it goes back to Israel.

Grace
You don't bring any blood sacrifice to the priest any more.
The blood of the animals, [Sacrifice] was a picture of Jesus.
These sacrifices were done away with when Jesus died. Jesus
is the sacrifice.
Note
We are saved by grace.
During the 1,000 year Reign, we will go back to the law and
have animal sacrifices.
And Jesus is setting on the Throne, in the Temple.

SHEEP

The sheep, picture of people. Psalms: 23:2 lead me by still
water; Sheep will not drink from water that is moving.

PAUL

Paul who wrote one third of the New Testament is
explaining the difference between, grace, and the law.

**These are the things you should be
learning in Sunday school**

IS GOD REAL IN YOUR LIFE?

God does not seem to be real, in people's lives.

What is the Bible all about?

What is God all about?

God wants to give you everything you want.

I will try to help you understand, some of these matters.

JESUS
Man or God?

God took on the form of man.
God put the seed into Mary and Jesus was born as man.
He did not act as God at any time.
If he wanted to be God, Mary would
have had nothing to do with it.
You cannot be man and God.
Sin enters in through one man, Adam.
Jesus died for Adam's sin.
Jesus was born into sin.
Adam was made with no sin.
Jesus died for Adam's sin.
Adam's sin = the world.
This is the story of Jesus.

When He rose from the grave by the
Father, then Jesus became God.
Jesus was seen by people everywhere as God, for forty days.
When He comes back, He will come
back as the All Mighty God.

Adam broke the law.
Jesus does not break the law.
Jesus was under the law; He was playing the role as man.
Jesus was a prophet.
Jesus was a priest.
Jesus was a king.
Jesus was the lamb.

Jesus was a judge.

Jesus was a servant.

Jesus was a teacher.

He taught the law and lives by the law.

Jesus prays to the Father to show you He came as Adam.

All the miracles Jesus did were done by
the prophets in the Old Testament.

Jesus came as the second Adam.

THE HOLY BIBLE
Authorized King James Version
66 books

39 in Old Testament 27 in the New Testament
This is the only Book in the world that changes people's lives.
The Bible tells how to live a life of
Blessing or the life of curses.
It is about rules and instructions
The Bible is about God, Jesus, and the Holy Spirit, love,
grace, hate, forgiving, wisdom, knowledge, the lost
and the Saved, Hell, and Heaven, judgment, prayer,
Priests, law, Israel, land and
The devil whose name is Lucifer.

There are only three sins and they are all are spelled [sin] in
the Bible.

[1] SIN The rejection of Jesus as God and, that He
died for you and, He was raised from the dead.
This is the only sin that gets you a ticket to hell.

[2] Sin Only the Saved can do this, it is called the
not Sin. This is what you are not doing for God.
God wants two hours and forty minutes a day of your time.

[3] sin Flesh, everything in our lives death
We all die because we all have sin in our lives, saved or lost.
The Bible is combined with all these things

You have to read the whole Bible to
understand what is going on.
You cannot read just half of it.

The understanding of the Bible and God does not come easily.
The churches today only spend four hours a week in church.
And some of them are thinking about cutting it down to three
hours a week. Do you think our kids would learn anything, if
they only went to school four hours a week?

Galatians: 6:7 Be not deceived; God is not mocked: for
whatsoever a man soweth, that shall he also reap.
8 For he that soweth to his flesh shall of the flesh reap
corruption; but he that soweth to the Spirit shall of the Spirit
reap life everlasting.

Isaiah 5:20 Woe unto them that call evil good, and good evil;
that put darkness for light, and light for darkness; that put
bitter for sweet, and sweet for bitter!
James 3:11 Doth a fountain send forth at the same place sweet
water and bitter?
Romans 6:1 What shall we say then? Shall we continue in sin,
that grace may abound?
2 God forbid. How shall we, that are dead to sin, live any
longer therein?

What God expects from you.
Let's get some things straight
God wants 10% of your money
Wrong
God wants 10% of your heart and He will
work with you on the other 90%
If I give God 10% of my money, He will take
care of me and everything in my life.
Wrong
If you give your heart to JESUS and be
obedient, He will take care of you.

Genesis 1:27 So God created man in his own
image, in the image of God created he him;
male and female created he them.
You want Love and attention
God wants the same
If I go to church, I will go to heaven
Wrong
Going to church has nothing to do with going to heaven
If you want to go to heaven .You have to repent of
your sins and ask Jesus to come into your heart.
Romans 10:9-13

A sign that you are going to Heaven is if you have a changed
life. You went from disobedient to obedient. It is what you do
outside of church. Not in church
St. Matthew 7:20 Wherefore by their fruits ye shall know
them.

21 Not every one that saith unto me, Lord, Lord, shall enter into the kingdom of heaven; but he that doeth the will of my Father which is in heaven.

22 Many will say to me in that day, Lord, Lord, have we not prophesied in thy name? and in thy name have cast out devils? and in thy name done many wonderful works?

23 And then will I profess unto them, I never knew you: depart from me, ye that work iniquity.

Here are the facts about you and God.

Jesus is waiting for you to ask him to forgive you of your sins and to come into your heart

Romans 10:9-13 when you do this you have an open line with Jesus.

You might say. Your wrong God answers my prayers all the time.

Wrong

God answered somebody else's prayers, somebody that has asked Him to come into their heart.

Another thing Jesus does. He fulfills all our needs, even if you are not saved.

Jesus did not answer your prayer, He fulfilled your need.

Another thing Jesus does. Every good thing you do in this life, Jesus repays you 10 times back whether you are lost or saved.

At judgment day you will not be able to point your finger in God's face and say I did this, where were you?

Jesus has all His bases covered.
You are the only one who can put yourself in Hell.
John 14:6 Jesus saith unto him, I am the way, the truth,
and the life: no man cometh unto the Father, but by me.

SOME MISCONCEPTIONS
ABOUT SIN AND HELL

God does not seem to be real in people's lives.

The biggest part of the blame falls on the misunderstanding of what some preachers are saying. The one word some don't have in their vocabulary is the word separation.

Sin is sin in their book. No, you have to separate the word sin.

Another word is the word Sabbath some say the first day of the week is the same as the seventh day of the week.

Some think Jesus can do what he wants because He is God. No. He is the Second Adam.

Some think anybody can be priests.

Some think the tribe of Levi and tribe Judah are the same.

You never can learn anything because you have to separate a lot of words in the Bible to get the understanding of God's Word.

Consequence is another word they don't have in their vocabulary What is the consequence for doing wrong?

GOD is keeping score on everybody. He knows how many hairs fall off your head each day.

The misunderstanding of why people go to hell.

Alcohol does not get you there.

Sex does not get you there.

Drugs do not get you there.

Gambling does not get you there

These things won't get you in hell

These things in your life **do not** bring happiness, joy, or peace in your life.

They bring sorrow, sadness, depression and all the other things that make life no good, so you are looking for the fulfillment in life in all the wrong places.

Jesus is the only way.

Jesus will give you all your wants in life; all you have to do is put as much time into GOD as you put into all of the above.

You only get out of it, what you put into it.

How do you get to hell?

It is all on you. You are the only one that can get you there.

You will not see any of your friends in hell. You will only see you, just you alone.

Luke 16:19-31

The rejection of Jesus Christ as God, the Son of God, and He died for you, He arose the third day and He is coming again.

This is the only thing that will get you into hell.

You say, I believe in all that, so does the devil and he trembles.

At judgment day every time, you heard about Jesus, and you turned away from Him, that is

What will put you in hell.

You got to accept Jesus as God, and that He died for you.

You have been eating of the apple that Adam ate, after you knew, right from wrong.

That's where it starts.

A change of life, and the more you learn about God, the more mud will be washed off.

The more God will bless you.

It is all about your time, obedience, the fear of the Lord, and faith.

STORIES ABOUT LIFE AND WHERE PREACHERS GO WRONG.

I smoked until somewhere around 1980. It was hard for me to quit. Some preacher said I was going to hell because I smoked. That is not in the Bible. Some preachers said I could not preach because I smoked.

In the song books there is a song, We Three Kings. None of this is in the Bible. No king or kings every came to see Jesus.

Jeremiah 10:21 For the pastors are become brutish, and have not sought the Lord: therefore they shall not prosper, and all their flocks shall be scattered.

Here are some other things that some
preachers do not have right.

No kings were there when Jesus was born.
The real story is about ten shepherds and 100 sheep. Luke 2 verses 8, 15, 18 and 20
Two years later the wise men came to the house. St. Matthew 2: verses 9 [young child] 10 and 11 [house]
What was The Mark of Cain? Genesis 4 verse 15
The Lord set a mark upon Cain, lest any finding him should kill him. [Baldness] Is 3:4
Baldness makes you feel naked. Adam & Eve sin and knew they were naked Gen. 3 verses 6 &7
Saturday & Sunday are not the same days in the Bible.

Nowhere in the Bible does it say, you cannot work on Sunday [Sunday the first day of week in the Bible]

The only sin that put you in hell is the rejection, of Jesus Christ as God and that he died for your sins.

Heaven and Hell

When you die you go one place or the other. All babies go to heaven when they die. When are you not a baby anymore? In this day and time it is hard to say. At one time it was around twelve years of age.

It is when they know right from wrong. That could be any time after five years of age.

It is important to start your kids in church when they are born. You have to answer for you.

Going to church does not get you to Heaven.

1Corinthians 2:14 But the natural man received not the things of the Spirit of God: for they are foolishness unto him: neither can he know them, because they are spiritually discerned.

Doing good works do not get you to Heaven.

Ephesian 2:8 For by grace are ye saved through faith; and that not of yourselves: it is the gift of God:

9 Not of works, lest any man should boast.

St. Matthew 25:41 Then shall he say also unto them on the left hand, Depart from me, ye cursed, into everlasting fire, prepared for the devil and his angels:

Romans 10:9 if thou shalt confess with thy mouth the Lord Jesus, and shalt believe in thine heart that God hath raised him from the dead, thou shalt be saved.

10 For with the heart man believeth unto righteousness; and with the mouth confession is made unto salvation.

Romans 6:23 for the wages of sin is death; but the gift of God is eternal life through Jesus Christ our Lord.

John 3:16 For God so loved the world, that he gave his only begotten Son, that whosoever believeth in him should not perish, but have everlasting life.

God is real in some people's lives.

You and sin, us going to hell

Luke 15:10 Likewise, I say unto you, there is joy in the presence of the angels of God over one sinner that repenteth.

The drunk said

"I am glad I asked Jesus to come into my life. I once was blind and now I can see. Jesus took that bad habit away from me".

The dope head said

"Thank you Jesus for being real in my life. The dope had ahold of my life until I found Jesus".

The gambler said

"I thank God for breaking that habit".

The prostitute said

"Jesus is the only way. Thank you Jesus for saving me."

The jail bird said

"Thank you Jesus for saving me. I have to spend the rest of my life in here. I am going to go to Bible school in here to help others."

I have been in a lot of church meetings, over the years. I have heard a lot of people stand up and thank Jesus for dying for them and they have come from all walks of life.

Hebrews: 10:31 It is a fearful thing to fall into the hands of the living God.

This is one thing; you have to do for yourself. You have to make your own choice, before you die. You know you are not happy and you are looking to fill that void in your life. You have tried everything and it is not working for you. My friend, stop running from God. You have just read, people's testimonies. Jesus is the way.

It is not about the preacher and it is not about the churches. It is about you and God.
It is about you.
One day you will stand in front of GOD. Just you will stand there all alone.

THE FLOOD

Genesis chapter 6 is where you read about why the Flood came to mankind. The world was full of violence. The last thing on the people's minds was God. Everybody was doing their own thing. It took 120 years to build the ark. Only 8 got on the ark Noah, his wife, their three sons, and their wives. They were on the ark for one year. God put the Rainbow in the sky as a sign, meaning not to flood the whole earth again.

The creation is found in Genesis chapter one.

A lot of people do not understand about the flood. They say, if it rains for forty days it will not flood the whole world. More than likely, they are right. So what is going on? To understand the flood you have to go back to the creation of the world. The Bible reads like this.

God created the heaven and the earth. The earth was without form, and void. The spirit of God moved upon the face of the waters. He made day and night the first day.

Note:
It never rained before the flood. God watered everything from the ground up.
The water that made the flood was created on the second day.

God said let there be a firmament in the midst of the waters and let it divide the waters from the waters.

God made the firmament and divided the waters which were under the firmament from the waters which were above the firmament.

Here is the key to the flood
God called the firmament Heaven.
Let the waters under the heaven be gathered together into one place and let the dry land appear.

We have water in the sky and one big piece of land below with water all around it.
God had rivers of water also.

Note:
God lets the water fall from heaven.
Genesis 7:11 windows of heaven were opened
Genesis 8:2 windows of heaven were closed
It fell so hard it broke up the land.
You should be able to see this by looking at a world atlas.

The Ark was like a log in the water, it was made to float.
All that water in the sky was like a filter, it filtered the sun's rays.
And man lived, to be over nine hundred years old.
After the flood the age drops to eighty years old.

Psalm 90: 10 KJV The days of our years are threescore years and ten; and if by reason of strength they be fourscore years, yet is their strength labour and sorrow; for it is soon cut off, and we fly away.

THE WOMAN RUNNING A WHORE HOUSE

God tells Joshua to send two spies to spy out the land of the city of Jericho. The two men went and stayed at a whore house ran by a woman name Rahab. They thought this was a good place to hide out. Well this plan did not last long, the king caught wind of this and sent men over there, to get the two men.

[Rahab] hid the two men, and tells the king's men they already left. And after they closed the gate, Rahab took the men to the roof and talked to them, "Rahab said "we have heard what happened. How the living God has taken care of all of you. I know your God has the power to overtake this land and the city of Jericho. I saved your life. I want you to save my life". The two men [spies] replied do not tell anybody we been here. Let us off the wall with a cord and we will let your family and everybody you are related to live. The spies said "Just put this cord in the window and we will take care of you." Rahab, did what the men said and all of her family and everybody that was a relative to her became saved.

This story is all about how God is real; He is the All Living God and All Powerful God.
This story also shows the proper fear of God and having faith.

All of this came by hearing of what God had done.
Faith comes by hearing.

Israel was a part of the story and saw everything God did.

Israel did not have any fear, or any faith. Israel did not believe God could do what He said He could do.

Israel walks around the mountain for forty years until they were all dead because of their lack of faith.

Looking through the eyes of the Lord, Rahab made Israel look real small.
Because of this fact, GOD richly blessed, Rahab

       She heard and believed and feared GOD.

THE END

This is the end of the Bible studies, hope you enjoyed them.

Hosea 4:6 my people are destroyed for lack of knowledge: because thou hast rejected knowledge, I will also reject thee, that thou shalt be no priest to me: seeing thou hast forgotten the law of thy God, I will also forget thy children.

There are some good preachers out there. They are just hard to find.
You have to accept Jesus as God and ask forgiveness, invite Him into your heart, and start a relationship with Him. You are born into Gods families as a little baby. Now you have to grow up to be an adult to take on the devil. Like any relationship, you have to spend a lot of time with it or it will not work.

I hope I have cleared up some things about God and what really is in the Bible.
Salvation is just a start of a new life. You have got to get real with God.
God will be real with you. You have to work it out with Him.

2Timmothy 2:15 study to show thyself approved unto God, a workman that needed not to be ashamed, rightly dividing the word of truth.

Each year that goes by you should know a little bit more. The church should be open 24/7 to help you through this with

God. But you can do this on your own. Nothing is impossible with God, all things are possible.

Mark 10:27 And Jesus looking upon them saith, With men it is impossible, but not with God: for with God all things are possible.

Mark 13:22 For false Christ and false prophets shall rise, and shall shew signs and wonders, to seduce, if it were possible, even the elect.

Keep your eyes on God and not the things of the world.

DAVID, A MAN AFTER GOD'S OWN HEART

David's life is a picture of what God is all about. How God deals with sin.
Before the story of Uriah and Bathsheba and after, Jesus said, David was a man after His own heart.

The twelve tribes of Israel wanted a king. God was against this because years later Jesus would be their king. Israel said, no we want to be like everybody else. We want a king now. So God said here are the rules and what you have to do when you have a king. Israel agreed to everything God said. Saul, from the tribe of Benjamin, was the first king.

Note:
    The twelve sons of Jacob were the blood line of the twelve tribes.

    Rachel died when she gave birth to Benjamin.

King Saul came against God's law, and God took the kingship from him.

God gave it to David.

David is from the tribe of Judah

Note:
    Jesus was from the tribe of Judah.

    He was Israel's King.

Israel had Jesus killed because He said He was their king.

David paid fourfold for what he did to Uriah and Bathsheba. Jesus said, that other than this act with Uriah and Bathsheba, that David was a man after His own heart.

You have to read the stories about David's life. You will find obedience, love, understanding, wisdom, kindness, joy, peace, and long suffering.

King Saul wanted David dead and ran David down like a dog would run down a rabbit.
David could have killed King Saul on two different occasions. He spared his life because he was God's anointed.

Uriah and Bathsheba were the only part of David's life that God was not pleased with.

David left God out of his life during this time.

THE LAW VERSUS THE PREACHERS

A lot of preachers believe Bathsheba took a bath in the late afternoon to entice David to have sex with her. The sex was so good that she got up and went home to an empty house. When she found out she was going to have a baby, she told David to have her husband come home. I will have sex with him so he will think it is his baby. Uriah would not have sex with his wife because of The Ark of the Covenant was in the field with his men. She told David the only thing you can do is to kill him and we will get married. David did and they got married and lived happy every after or at least Bathsheba did.

David repented and paid fourfold. Bathsheba did not repent and got blessed by God.

She was among the top ten most blessed women in the Bible. She never repented for having sex with David she demanded that David make her son the next king.

Note
David had two sons Absalom and Adonijah who was upset because God took the kingship from them and gave it to Bathsheba's son, Solomon, for having sex with their Dad, David.

This is what a lot of the preachers believe happened. I cannot change their mind.

I have tried for thirty years. Sending out letters to six hundred preachers and talking, face to face, with everybody that knows this story.

I told them, you are opening up to many wrong doors.

This is what I get out of this story, the way the preachers were teaching it.

Bathsheba is the only woman in the Bible who never answered for her sin.
Bathsheba was the only wife out of seven that had sex before marriage.
A married man having sex with a married woman is ok.
It is ok to have sex before marriage.
Open marriage is ok. David and Bathsheba did it.
Killing is ok if you are covering up your sin.
Only David paid for the sin. Bathsheba got blessed.

John 8:1 -11
A lot of preachers believe because they did not bring the man, the man did not have to answer to God for what he had done.

When Jesus wrote on the ground, the preachers believe Jesus was writing to the mad crowd.

The story of Judas having Jesus arrested.

A lot of preachers think it was about the money and to have Jesus killed.

This is what the preachers are saying.

This is what the law says.
You have to understand the Law before you can understand a lot of the Bible stories.
God wrote the Law.
Deuteronomy 22:22 KJV If a man be found lying with a woman married to an husband, then they shall both of them die, both the man that lay with the woman, and the woman: so shalt thou put away evil from Israel.
David and Bathsheba,
It looks like God is coming against his own Law. The preachers preach the story that way.
The law never changes. The preachers are not looking at the law. They are looking at the way man would look at it. There is man's way and there is God's way, which is the Law
The Jewish Law said both will die for this act of adultery.
Most preachers cannot explain why Bathsheba is one of the most blessed women in the Bible. The preachers think she committed adultery, which is against God's Law.
Bathsheba did not break any of God's laws

In John 8:1-11, The Pharisees bring a Gentile woman to Jesus for committing adultery. She is not under the Jewish law. She is under the Roman law. There is no law against adultery in the Roman law.
Some preachers cannot explain where is the man?

It looks like God is only taking care of half the problem.
The Jewish law reads both will die for this act of adultery.
God never takes care of half the problem and He never breaks any of His laws.

The story of David and Bathsheba and the story of the woman taken in adultery are all about the Law.
These stories in the Bible just did not make any sense to me. The way the preachers were telling the story did not make any sense either. In Bible school, they told it the same way all the preachers were telling it. I kept telling them, this couldn't be right. They would end up saying; God does not tell us everything. So I started asking God about all of these Bible stories that did not make sense to me. I got nothing from God. Every time I hear a preacher preach on these stories, I said, "God; this just does not make sense."

The woman in John 8-1:11 got caught in the very act of adultery. Where is the man? They did not bring the Jewish man who was caught in the very act of adultery.

Besides these two stories, another story that confused me was the story of Judas. What was Judas thinking about?
He brought back the money.
Judas and the rest of the Disciples had a misunderstanding about the way Jesus was going to set up his kingdom.
Judas never dreamt about them killing Jesus.
Jesus was to overthrow the Roman Government.
Twenty years after I graduated from Bible school, God told me and showed me in the Bible what these stories are all about.

DAVID AND BATHSHEBA

DAVID AND BATHSHEBA

II Samuel 11: 1-27

David came home from the battle. He left his men on the battle field. This was not the proper protocol for a king. Everybody was supposed to come home together. David crept into town, only the people in the palace, knew he was home. He told everyone he was tired and was going to bed. He climbed off of his bed, went to the roof, and looked down onto Bathsheba. He lusted after her. She was taking a bath, unaware that David was watching her. David couldn't take it any longer. He went down, and asked "who the woman next door was?"

"They told him Bathsheba, the wife of Uriah."

Uriah, was one of the Generals, in David's army

David told them to bring her to him just as she was. He wanted her brought to his private quarters.

They thought it was strange that David was doing all of these things. They had to do what the king said. There was a knock on Bathsheba's door, she put a towel around her and went to the door. The king wants to see you right now. Let me get dressed. I will be ready in a minute. No, come just as you are. Thinking that her husband might be dead, she did what they said. They took her to David's private quarters. David jerks the towel off her and rapes her. After it was over, she went home crying.

Bathsheba was thinking what was this all about? He had seven wives.

She discovered she was with child.

She sent a letter, telling David she was going to have a baby.

David called her husband from the war to see him. David asked "Uriah, how is the war going?" Uriah said, "I believe, if we charge, at full strength, we can win." He was honored that David asked him the question. David said go on down to your house and have some time with your wife for two or three days, then come back. I will give you a note to take back to the Commanding General. The next day, David found Uriah sleeping at his door. David asked, "Uriah what are you doing?"

Uriah said, "I cannot have sex with my wife. The Ark of God is out there with my men, I fear God. I would be doing wrong."

David said to Uriah. "Come on in, spend the day with me, and we will talk. We will have a few drinks and have a good time together."

When the evening came, Uriah was feeling pretty good.

David said to Uriah, "Go on down, have some fun with your wife for two or three days and come back. I will give you a note to take to the commanding General." The next day, David found Uriah, at the door again.

David asked Uriah, "What are you doing?"

Uriah said, "I cannot go and be with my wife. That is wrong, not right."

David said, "Go back to the battle and take this note."

The note read, "Make sure Uriah dies today and send word, to let me know when it is done." The note came back, Uriah was dead.

Note: The Enemy was mocking God because they had killed one of David's top generals.

They thought their god was better than David's God.

David sent a note back; command them to charge them at full strength. They did and won the war.

Just after Bathsheba got over the death of her husband, David sent a note to Bathsheba. The note, read, "I want to marry you."

She wrote back, "No that is not going to happen." A month later, David sent another note asking her to marry him. She said, "If you make my son the next King, I will marry you."

David sent for her saying, it will be done. Your son will be the next King. Just after Bathsheba's third son was born, the first born baby fell ill. God told David, the child would die because of the way you let Uriah die. The child would not die because of the way he was conceived.

God said, "The Enemy is mocking me and saying their god is bigger than me." They were having a party.

David prayed and did not eat. He was hoping God would change His mind. The child died. David went in onto Bathsheba, and she conceived Solomon. Solomon was Bathsheba's fourth son. God said, "Solomon would take the place of the child that died; Solomon would be the next king."

THE FINAL OUTCOME
OF THIS STORY

DAVID REPENTED

When David was a young man, he kept his dad's sheep. He did this for many years. David knew all about sheep. When, Nathan told David the story about the man who had sheep, David could relate to the story and he got mad when he heard the man took the only lamb the farmer had. David said he will die and pay fourfold. Nathan said, you are the man, David. David repented to the Lord.

God showed David Grace and told David you will not die but you will pay fourfold. You did this secretly but you will pay openly.

THE KINGSHIP

David asked Bathsheba to marry him. Bathsheba said no. David you raped me and killed my husband. Now you want me to marry you. David was feeling the guilt of what he had done to Bathsheba. David told Bathsheba that what he had done was wrong. I want to marry you. Bathsheba said, for the wrong you did the only way, I would marry you is if my boy that you're the daddy of through rape, will be the next king. David said he will be the next king and if anything were to happen to the boy, the kingship will stay with you and will not come back to any of my other wives and their sons.

Note: The baby did die at the age of three. Bathsheba had her fourth son right after the child died and his name was Solomon. God said he would be the next king.

Back to the story

David called all of the family in and, told the family, what he had done to Bathsheba. All of the wives and boys were shocked and understood. Bathsheba should have the kingship rights.

Note: The kingship rights come by the order the sons were born in starting with the first born and going down the line.

1Chronicles 3:1-9 KJV Now these were the sons of David, which were born unto him in Hebron; the firstborn Amnon, of Ahinoam the Jezreelitess; the second Daniel, of Abigail the Carmelitess: {Daniel: or, Chileab}
2 The third, Absalom the son of Maachah the daughter of Talmai king of Geshur: the fourth, Adonijah the son of Haggith:
3 The fifth, Shephatiah of Abital: the sixth, Ithream by Eglah his wife.
4 These six were born unto him in Hebron; and there he reigned seven years and six months: and in Jerusalem he reigned thirty and three years.
5 And these were born unto him in Jerusalem; Shimea, and Shobab, and Nathan, and Solomon, four, of Bathshua the

daughter of Ammiel: {Shimea: or, Shammua} {Bathshua: or, Bathsheba} {Ammiel: or, Eliam}

6 Ibhar also, and Elishama, and Eliphelet, {Elishama: also called, Elishua}

7 And Nogah, and Nepheg, and Japhia,

8 And Elishama, and Eliada, and Eliphelet, nine. {Eliada: or, Beeliada}

9 These were all the sons of David, beside the sons of the concubines, and Tamar their sister.

Absalom and Adonijah came to their dad and said this is not right; we are being punished for something we did not do. David tried to reason with them, David saw he was not going any place with this and said, "It is what it is."

A few years later Absalom went and talked to his dad and said I do not think I should have lost the kingship because of your foolishness. I am taking the kingship away from you. David tried to reason with Absalom but Absalom did not want to hear it. Absalom said, it is what it is. Absalom went out and took the kingship away from his dad. A few years later, Absalom died and the kingship went back to David.

Adonijah knew Solomon was going to be king after David died. Abonijah tried to take the kingship from his dad two days before David died, thinking Solomon would have to wait until he died before Solomon would be king. Bathsheba found out what was going on with Abonijah and put a stop to it. Solomon was the next king.

DAVID PAID FOURFOLD

Three years after David raped Bathsheba, God sent [Nathan, the prophet,] to tell David a parable. II Samuel 12: 1-25

Nathan told David, you are the man in the parable.

2Samuel 12:1 And the LORD sent Nathan unto David. He came unto him and said unto him, there were two men in one city; the one rich, and the other poor.
David was the rich man and Uriah was the poor man.

2 The rich man had exceeding many flocks and herds:
David had 7wives and concubines.

3 But the poor man had nothing, save one little ewe lamb, which he had bought and nourished up: and it grew up together with him, and with his children; it did eat of his own meat, and drank of his own cup, and lay in his bosom, and was unto him as a daughter.
Uriah's wife, Bathsheba, was innocent. [One little ewe lamb]

4 And there came a traveler unto the rich man, and he spared to take of his own flock and of his own herd, to dress for the wayfaring man that was come unto him; but took the poor man's lamb, and dressed it for the man that was come to him.

The desire of the flesh came [traveler] unto David who had seven wives and David took Uriah's wife, innocent Bathsheba to fulfill the desires of the flesh.

David repents, for what he had done. God spared his life, but he paid fourfold.

Here are some things that happened to David after God told David that he would pay fourfold and Bathsheba's baby will be the next king

The first born baby of Bathsheba died; Solomon will be the next king Bathsheba's fourth son.

Amnon First son of David   1Chronicles 3:1
Amnon raped Tamar his sister. Absalom killed him, for raping his sister, Tamar.
II Samuel chapter 13

Absalom   Deuteronomy 22:25
Absalom was David third son.   I Chronicles 3:2
Absalom knew the kingship was Solomons, after David was dead. Absalom became king, while David was still alive.
2Samuel 15:10 But Absalom sent spies throughout all the tribes of Israel, saying, As soon as ye hear the sound of the trumpet, then ye shall say, Absalom reigned in Hebron.

Adonijah
Adonijah was David fourth son.   I Chronicles 3:2
Adonijah knew the kingship was Solomon's after David was dead.

Adonijah's game plan was that he would become king, just before David died. Adonijah thought that Solomon would then have to wait until he died to become king. Bathsheba stopped this game plan.   I Kings 1:1-53

Bathsheba, herself said she was not a whore.
1Kings 1:21 Otherwise it shall come to pass, when my lord the king shall sleep with his fathers, that I and my son Solomon shall be counted offenders.
The word offenders means whore and the son of a whore.
Adonijah said to Bathsheba " God took the kingship from me and gave it to you because David raped you "
1Kings 2:15 And he said, Thou knowest that the kingdom was mine, and that all Israel set their faces on me, that I should reign: howbeit the kingdom is turned about, and is become my brother's: for it was his from the Lord.

BATHSHEBA

Some preachers lead you to believe that Bathsheba was at fault because they believed she enticed David to have sex with her. The law said Bathsheba was not guilty Deuteronomy 22:25
In the case of rape, Bathsheba did not break any laws.
This is why she never had to account for having sex with David.
Here is the story of Bathsheba that shows her innocence.
Bathsheba was the wife of Uriah. David killed Uriah for taking a stand for the Lord.
II Samuel 11: 11

All of David's wives were beautiful women. David was the man that all women dreamed about. David had it all. The only woman that did not run after David was Bathsheba.

2Samuel 11:27 and when the mourning was past, David sent and fetched her to his house, and she became his wife, and bare him a son. But the thing that David had done displeased the Lord.

It does not say that what David and Bathsheba had done that displeased the Lord.

2Samuel 12:9 Wherefore hast thou despised the commandment of the Lord, to do evil in his sight? thou hast killed Uriah the Hittite with the sword, and hast taken his wife to be thy wife, and hast slain him with the sword of the children of Ammon. [low class army]

There was no love here, yet David had four sons by Bathsheba. 1Chronicles 3:5 And these were born unto him in Jerusalem; Shimea, and Shobab, and Nathan, and Solomon, four, of Bathsheba the daughter of Ammiel:

You can see Bathsheba had no part in this sex act.
She was pure from this sex act. 2Samuel 11:4 for she was purified from her uncleanness:
David sent messengers and took her, she did not come willingly. She was taking a bath. She came to the door with just a towel around her. The guards did not even let her get dressed. Let me get dressed. No, "come as you are". She questioned, "Just a towel?" The guards said "Yes".
The king said, "Just as you are."
David jerks the towel off and raped her.

After she was raped she went home. 2Samuel 11:4 and she returned unto her house.

Deuteronomy 22:25 But if a man find a betrothed damsel in the field, and the man force her, and lie with her: then the man only that lay with her shall die

That is why Bathsheba never had to repent for this act.
This is why her son would be the next king.
I will only become your wife, if my son, the result of the rape,will be the next king.
David called all of his wives [seven of them] and their boys. David said " Bathsheba's son will be the next king" At that time, the boy's name was Shimea or Shammua, Bathsheba's first born.
This boy became sick at 3 years old and died. Then God told David her fourth son, Solomon would be king.

WOMAN TAKEN IN ADULTERY

Gentiles are not under the Jewish laws. They wanted Jesus to throw the first stone so they could accuse him of her murder.

This story is found in the New Testament.

WOMAN TAKEN IN ADULTERY

There is a lot of confusion about this story.

JEWISH LAW VERSUS ROMAN LAW

John 8:1-11 The man's name and the woman's name were not given in this story.

A lot of people believe that God only took care of half the problem.

Jesus never said anything about the man.

She was caught in the very act of adultery.

If you break the law of adultery, the law said, both will be stoned to death.

The Pharisees knew the law by heart.

They were the group of people that brought the woman to Jesus.

This was the key to the story.

They did not want Jesus to stone her; they just wanted Jesus to throw the first rock.

Jesus was talking to a small group of people. This group of people knew the law.

These are the facts, here is the story.

The Pharisees brought this young girl butt naked to Jesus. They told Jesus they caught her in the very act of adultery. Because the woman was standing there naked, scared to death, shaking like a leaf, Jesus took what they said as the truth. Because of the different ages in this group, she had to be the biggest whore in town, who everybody knew and she did not say anything. She knew she was guilty.

Thinking she was going to be stoned to death because the Pharisees said she should be stoned. Because they knew she was a Gentile and did not fall under the Jewish law, they wanted Jesus to cast the first rock.

They would do the rest. Everybody knew she was a Gentile and she was whoring around with Jewish men.

That was why they said, she should be stoned.

If they would have brought the man, she would have fallen under the Jewish law, but they would have had to kill them both.

They could have stoned both of them where they got caught in adultery. They did not have to bring her in front of Jesus.

That is another reason why, I believe she is a gentile.

There was no law under the Roman law that said you can kill somebody for having sex with married men.

Jesus would have been charged with murder for casting the first rock.

The only one, who did not know that they did not have a case, was the woman.

Thinking Jesus was going to cast the first rock, Jesus stooped down and wrote to her in the sand. It is O.K. I will take care of this.

Jesus stood up and said, He that is without any sin, cast the first rock.

The group of people who Jesus was talking to stood up and looked at them

and they knew they could not take this any further.

The group of people could bring charges against them and they could end up in jail.

They left mad, one by one, telling the woman a few words as they passed by her.

Jesus said, where are the accusers? The woman said, there are none, Lord.

When she said Lord, she became saved, through faith, that Jesus was who he said he was the son of God. I am your God now; keep your eyes on me. She left happy, she knew the Lord.

JUDAS AND
JESUS ARREST

JUDAS

Judas was chosen by Jesus to be his disciple. He was the treasurer for Jesus.

Judas had all the money.

A lot of people thought that it was all about the money. The money had no more to do with it, than the kiss did.

It was not about the kiss and it was not about the money; otherwise, he would have not brought the money back.

It was about the power.

The thirty pieces of silver was a token, or we could say it was a contract between the High Priest and Judas. The high amount of money was a symbol of a strong contract. This was between the two of them. Nobody else could say it was their idea. This was all on Judas. This is what the money was all about.

The plan was to switch the power from Jesus to himself. .

When John the Baptist died, the wheels started turning.

The high Priest could not do anything while John the Baptist was alive.

Judas was just waiting for John the Baptist to die.

You would have been a dead man, if you came against John the Baptist.

King Herod [King of Judea] [Israel] had John the Baptist put in jail because that was what King Herod's wife begged him to do.

[Note:] Rome allowed Israel to have their own government within their Roman government as long the Romans controlled the people.

John the Baptist was preaching about the sins in King Herod and his wife's life.

John the Baptist did not break any laws, to tell of it the law he broke was something like spitting where people walk he could be released at any time.

MARK 6:14 - 28

The wife of King Herod wanted John the Baptist dead. Here is what she did to make that happen.

[The wife of King Herod told her daughter to dance for the king and make it as sexy as you can and when the king asks you what you want, tell him, John the Baptist's head in a charger]

[On a platter] She did, the king did not want to put John in jail and he did not want to kill him. But he could not go back on his word. The king offered half of his kingdom, She said no, I just want John the Baptist's head.

JOHN THE BAPTIST

John's mother was cousins with Jesus mother Mary. John was six months older than Jesus.

John preached for six months. Jesus and John died the same year.

When Jesus was baptized by John, Israel was in a new arrangement. Instead of bringing a blood sacrifice (animal), you now had to repent for your sins. (Grace)

The Priesthood as whole did not go along with this. This is why the Priest wanted Jesus dead.

John passed the Priesthood over to Jesus from the tribe of Judah. The Priests are from the levitical priesthood.

Read Hebrews 7:11-14 New Testament

You had to come from the blood line of Aaron in order to be a Priest and from the tribe of Levi

If you are from the blood line of Moses you could wait on the Priest.

Jesus was the high Priest; I believe the disciples were from the tribe of Levi, the blood line of Moses because they waited on Jesus

Back to the story

Everything had to be in the right place to get this to come off just right.

Lucifer had been waiting for four thousand years, for this one moment in his life.

The blood was flowing, one thousand miles a minute, the all-time high. Nothing could go wrong,

Judas thought Jesus was going to set up his KINGDOM and I am the man responsible for it. Jesus did not set up His Kingdom.

The all-time high became the all-time low. Judas was mad, upset, confused, and depressed. With his chin dragging on the ground, he took the money back. The contract was over. Sad and broken hearted, he thought Jesus would throw him under the bus.

Because Judas, plan was to over throw the Roman Government. Not to have Jesus killed.

He did not want to be beat to death by the Roman soldiers like Jesus was. So he knew, he was going to die. So he went and killed himself. The dream became a nightmare.

Are you dreaming about going to heaven or do you know for sure that you are going to heaven?

Do not be like Judas and let your dream become your nightmare.

JESUS

The Roman Government took over Israel.

The Priest went to Pontius Pilate and said "we want to go by the Law of Moses."

The Priest read the law to Pilate. Pilate agreed to their law, but they had to come to him and tell him what law was broken. He then would tell them, you can kill this person for breaking your law. This kept everybody on the same page. Nobody is dying without cause. Israel could not just kill people.

Jesus was kissed and arrested. The High Priest took Jesus to Pontius Pilate. Pilate was the Governor. Pilate asked, which law, of the laws of Moses, did Jesus break?

The High Priest said "Jesus did not break any Laws,"

Pilate said. "What is it that you want?"

The Priest said, "We want you to kill Him."

Pilate asked, "What Law did Jesus break?"

The Priest said, "No law"

Pilate said, "I have to have a law that Jesus broke before I kill him."

High Priest of Israel said, "We want Him dead."

Pilate said, "There is a law that I can release someone. Who do you want to let go?

Do you want to release Jesus, who was innocent or Barabbas, who had broken all the laws?"

The Priest said, "We want the man who had broken all the laws. We want Barabbas released."

This was not what Judas wanted.

This was where Judas wanted Jesus to set up His kingdom and over throw the Roman government.

It did not happen.

If somebody had found out that Pilate had killed a man who had not broken any laws, Pilate himself would have been put to death.

Pilate was not going to kill Jesus. He had not broken any laws.

The Priest said, "Jesus said He was our king".

Pilate asked the Priest, "Where is his army? What country does he rule?"

The Priest, "Ask Jesus. He will tell you."

Pilate asked, "What do you have to say for yourself, Jesus?"

Jesus did not say anything.

Pilate said, "Jesus has no country or army so I do not think He is your king. This man is thirty three years old; No, Jesus will not be put to death."

The Priest said, "Caesar is our king. We will go to Caesar."

Pilate had to do what they wanted when Israel said they would go to Caesar.

Pilate, said, "I wash my hands of this. The blood of Jesus will be on Israel's hands and not Rome's."

Israel said, "Kill Jesus."

Pilate said, "Jesus is your King. I will write it on Jesus cross for everyone to see."

Pilate wrote, "Jesus of Nazareth, King of the Jews."

He wrote it in Hebrew, Greek, and Latin.

The high Priest said, "No, no, do not put that on the cross."

Pilate said, "If you want the man dead, this is the way it will be done."

And Israel said, "Kill Jesus, kill Jesus."

Note:

Pilate knew of the miracles Jesus had done. It was the talk of the town.

Pilate knew Jesus was doing more good than harm.

Note:

Because the Roman government allowed a government within a government, Pilate had to keep an eye on everything Israel did. Pilate had officers reporting to him things that got the people stirred up whether it was happy, sad, mad, or a lot of noise. Pilate stayed on top of everything.

It was reported to him.

John was baptizing in the river and when John baptized Jesus, the talk was that Jesus would be the last Priest and was from the tribe of Judah.

This is one of the reasons; they wanted Jesus dead because Jesus was not a Levite.

Hebrews chapter 7 verses 11 – 14

Another reason the Priests wanted Jesus dead, the priest was making money hand over fist in the temple. Jesus put a stop to this by kicking them out and turning over the tables. The

priest could not open this back up until Jesus died. Jesus was only 33 years of age. It was not happening tomorrow.
Matthew chapter 21 verses 12 and 13.

Jesus said He was their King.
The Priest really was not mad or upset about that.
If that was the case, they would have had Jesus arrested a week earlier when Jesus rode into town on an ass and everybody was saying Jesus, our King, our Priest and the Son of God.

John chapter 12 verses: 12- 15.
Pilate knew all of this when the priest said they would go to Caesar. Pilate had to do what they said or it would have cost him his life.

Now you know the true story of the death of Jesus. He laid His life down for you.

This is the Lamb that laid down His life for you. He was God, who could have stopped this at any time. Jesus paid for Adam's sin.
Sin entered into the world by one Man's sin, Adam [who was made with no sin]
Jesus, who had no sin, was born into sin [Adam's sin.]

Because of Adam's sin we are all born into sin, our nature is to do wrong.

We are accountable for our sins when we reach the age of knowing right from wrong which could be from 5 to 12 years old.

All babies go to haven when they die.

EVERYBODY WANTS TO KNOW ABOUT THE ANTI-CHRIST.

There are a lot of different views on this subject. I have my own views on this matter.

Here is what God has shown me.

There will not be planes crashing, or cars running into other cars.

The Anti-Christ is coming to be worshipped as the Almighty God.

Jesus came as the second Adam; the devil is coming as the return of Christ.

The devil will come as the Lord in darkness.

Amos 5:20 Shall not the day of the Lord be darkness, and not light? even very dark, and no brightness in it?

1Thessalonians 5:2 for yourselves know perfectly that the day of the Lord so cometh as a <u>thief</u> in the night.

Jesus had a reason to come to earth and that was to die for Adam's sin. [The world's sins]

The devil does not have those intentions.

The devil will come as the Almighty God.
He already has the world in his back pocket.

Amos 5:18
18 Woe unto you that desire the day of the Lord! To what end
is it for you? The day of the Lord is darkness, and not light.
The Anti- Christ, the devil himself, will be coming, as Jesus.
For seven years, the five I wills come into play.
Isaiah 14:12 How art thou fallen from heaven, O Lucifer, son
of the morning! how art thou cut down to the ground, which
didst weaken the nations!

Isaiah 14:13 For thou hast said in thine heart, I will ascend
into heaven, I will exalt my throne above the stars of God: I
will sit also upon the mount of the congregation, in the sides
of the north:
14 I will ascend above the heights of the clouds; I will be like
the most High.

The devil is God's highest ranked angel.
He will come with all the power that God has given him.

John 14:30 KJV Hereafter I will not talk much with you: for
the prince of this world cometh, and hath nothing in me.

Here is the story.
The rapture takes place. The Anti-Christ will tell you, we have
to mark everybody for we have lost a lot of people in all this.

The mark will get you free food, all bills paid, and you will be healed from all diseases. You are going to think he is God. There will be two [witnesses] telling the world that he is not God and 144,000 preachers in Israel preaching that he is not God. The world will kill these preachers after three and a half years.

It does not matter what is going on.

Darkness will take over. If they are blowing up the world with bombs, darkness will settle it down.

Think about it, there is a whole lot of power in Darkness.

Read the story of the ten virgins St. Matthew: 25-1 to 10

This story talks about Jesus coming in darkness.

There will be a man who will be the spokesperson for Lucifer. This will happen just like Moses and God. He will be about eighty years of age. This man will be handpicked by Lucifer. As Moses explains the things God wanted them to know.

This man will explain the things Lucifer wants you to know. [False Prophet]

The spirit of God will come on the two witnesses and 144.000 preachers.

You will find these facts in the book of Revelation.

The father of Lies will be here. [Satan]

John 8:44 Ye are of your father the devil, and the lusts of your father ye will do. He was a murderer from the beginning, and abode not in the truth, because there is no truth in him. When he speaketh a lie, he speaketh of his own: for he is a liar, and the father of it. [king James]

Here is an example of an illusion, often called a magic trick.
Illusion = lie.
The man shows you an empty box. Then the man puts a big rabbit in the box. The man waves a stick over it and the man shows you the box and the rabbit is not in the box. The man just showed you an Illusion. Where is the rabbit?
There was a mirror in the box. You only saw half the box and it looked like the whole box was empty. The man put the rabbit behind the mirror in the box and the box looks like it is empty. The man showed you a lie.

The illusion is that Lucifer is going to come as Jesus.

The whole world will worship him as God.

Lucifer will take care of your debt, if you just take the mark which is 666.
You will think he is God because that is what the whole world is looking for.
This is what he will copy.
Am 5:18 Woe unto you that desire the day of the LORD! To what end is it for you? the day of the LORD is darkness, and not light.
20 Shall not the day of the Lord be darkness, and not light? even very dark, and no brightness in it? [King James]

SOMETHING YOU MIGHT WANT TO THINK ABOUT.

THIS IS WHAT THE REST OF
THE WORLD IS SAYING.

Google
Last Pope

Google
Monster power drink
Go to [monster energy drinks are works of the Satan]

Google
Disney and 666

Things of Interest

The same people who took prayer out of schools are the same people after 9-11 standing on the steps of the Lincoln memorial that said, let's pray. What is wrong with this picture?

The same people that tell you Jesus is not God are the same people that use His name in vain.
Even Hollywood uses it a lot in their movies. What is wrong with this picture?

Let me tell you a story that someone told me.

There was a man who had a lot of money. He worked long hours each day. Six days a week.

He had a sports car he drove every Sunday about four hours a day, on a dirt road that was about thirty miles long with two big curves in it. He would drive it as fast as he could. The road was not traveled that much. You hardly ever saw a car. He was driving his car one Sunday, In one of the curves he saw a car coming at him in his lane. He was doing all he could do to keep from hitting the car. As the car came by, he saw that it was a woman driver. He was mad because the car was in his lane, she said with a loud voice "PIG". He called her every name in the book when she said that. He thought she was calling him a pig. He was so hot about what was going on, you could have cooked an egg in the car. He got his car under control. He saw a PIG in the road.

What he thought was going on, had nothing to do with what was really going on.

The same goes for the Bible. Most people do not get the whole story before they really know what is going on.

PROVERBS

The book of Proverbs is the book in the Bible that tells you all about life and the ways of people.
What to do and what not to do and the outcome, if you do them. It is the book you should have under your pillow. You will look at things differently. If you get depressed about

something or mad at somebody, this is the book to read. I would say it covers all walks of life.

THE GAP
IN THE CHURCHES TODAY

In today's world there are a lot more empty pews at church. Some preachers have stopped feeding the Lambs and the sheep, meaning we don't go to church to glorify God, or learn His ways. Church is supposed to be encouraging and uplifting. Churches are having a hard time succeeding in this. Currently, people 50 years of age or younger do not seem to think church is important. Eventually, when the older generation dies, the churches will be empty.

Hebrews 10:31 It is a fearful thing to fall into the hands of the living God.

FOR PEOPLE WHO STUDY THE BIBLE

ABRAHAM'S BLESSING IN A NUT SHELL

Abraham Genesis 12:1-2

Isaac Genesis 17:19

Jacob Genesis 27:22-23

Israel Genesis 35:10

Ephraim Genesis 48:14-20

1 Chronicles 5:1

Judah Psalms 78:67-68

Note read the book of Hosea
To find out why God took it from
Ephraim and gave it to Judah

Isaiah 11:1-14

Genesis 49:8-12

Genesis 12:2
Everybody who is saved and saved by grace

Galatians 4:28

Galatians 3:14

Note: read the book of Ephesians
To learn about the Gentiles

NOTE FROM THE AUTHOR

The Bible is not a book you can pick up and understand what you read. It was Witten by God. God will only give you the understanding in His time. First you have to be saved to get the understanding.

There is prophesying about the life of Jesus in all of the Old Testament, bits and pieces here and there.

God wrote the law and He follows it frontwards and backwards.

When you are reading the story, keep in mind the law. This is the culture of the Book.

In the Bible the people are reading the law, following the law, breaking the law, ignoring the law, playing with the law, or teaching the law. You have to get a basic understanding of the law to understand the Bible. Do not get discouraged when you read the Bible. If you stay at it, God will give it to you.

When you go to church the preacher might preach on what you have been reading in the Bible or maybe the Sunday school lesson will be about something you read. Pray before you read your Bible and ask God to give you the understanding of what you are about to read, Sometimes God gives you the understanding right away. Sometimes He gives it to you in a week or two. Even if it is years later, God will bring it to your mind when you need it. God's time is right.

Printed in the United States
By Bookmasters